Advance Praise

"Often as poets start putting their work out, they can be watchful, each passage like a step down a rain-wet road. Or one can throw aside caution, write poems to the soundtrack of 'purple meteors' crashing away. Kashiana can move into an opiate's persona, where she is 'erased of light', her body a furnace. Kashiana's voice will haunt readers for a long while."

> — Keki N. Daruwalla
> Author, Padma Shree and Sahitya Akademi awardee

"Kashiana Singh's transcendent collection of poems *Woman by the Door* is a powerful journey between the liminal spaces that inhabit the bodies—physical, emotional, intuition, spiritual, and divine alive in Woman, as she stands "stubborn in the south-east corner of [her] body." Walk back and forth between these doors, and discover yourself on the vibrant threshold of your own transformation."

> — Kai Coggin
> Poet, Author and Teaching Artist

"In *Woman by the Door* Kashiana Singh first stands in the doorway observing with self-awareness and nostalgic love and longing "childhood season's first mango offered in prayer fragrant mornings I can still taste." This wise poet shows us how detours are not always inconveniences or time-wasters but may lead to new opportunities and discoveries. Her collection provides something of a template for how to live a fully examined, worthy life, as Socrates would have prescribed."

> — Betsy Mars
> Author, Photographer and Editor

"Singh's eye is attuned to the subtle, such as catching the shadows of fingers on egg white walls. Live! is the dominant note in the poems. She pays tribute to her cultural matrix peopled with and honoring the activities of mothers, fathers, grandfathers and grandmothers elevated to poetry.

I am a pitcher of iced sherbet, a keeper of sticky memories, she avers, while she does something quite extraordinary—her poetry unapologetically is simmered in home spices, fusing the art of cooking, and the being of womanhood to language."

— Usha Akella
Poet, Creative Ambassador City of Austin, Founder – Matwaala

"*Woman by the Door* is a pursuit of belonging, birth and death. Eloquence, mystery, beauty, rage, empathy, joy, sorrow, artful use of language yet a free flow of swelling passion pervades the poems. Kashiana is at her peak; she is here to plunge into the gyres of human existence and own its gore and glory."

— Jhilam Chattaraj
Academic and Poet

"An endless reflection on memory, experience, and travel, simmering in the image, bursting with emotion, *Woman by the Door* sings a very particular tune, and yet casts a wide harmony through Singh's precise selection of word, elegant display of linguistic code-switching, and her willingness to be true to herself and her experiences, no matter the cost."

— Kiran Bhat
Author, Polyglot and Traveler

Woman by the Door

Woman by the Door

Kashiana Singh

Apprentice
House Press
Loyola University Maryland

First Edition

Paperback ISBN: 978-1-62720-404-0
Ebook ISBN: 978-1-62720-405-7

Printed in the United States of America

Design by: Hope Pinsonault
Edited by Claire Winterling
Promotion plan by Erin Hurley

Published by Apprentice House Press

Apprentice House Press
Loyola University Maryland
4501 N. Charles Street
Baltimore, MD 21210
410.617.5265
www.ApprenticeHouse.com
info@ApprenticeHouse.com

For the living poem I am blessed with –
my
grandson
Kabir
my heart is at its fullest

Also by Kashiana Singh

Shelling Peanuts and Stringing Words
Crushed Anthills

Contents

APERTURES

An aperture is the diaphragm of the lens that controls

how much light passes through into the camera.

Homesick

alphonso
bearing the legacy
of colonization

basant
an edible canopy of
fiery blossoms

fallen mangoes
I bottle pickles
in opaque jars

scorching sun
serpentine rows
of tangy green

childhood
season's first mango
offered in prayer

fragrant mornings
I can still taste a
simmering chutney

summer nights
endless stories
and mangoes

My favorite scenes

My favorite scenes are
where childhood is drawn inside
cross-legged places, our oiled hair
floor length, braided patiently into
a warp and weft of tight caution, ends
ribboned by mama into crescent bows

My favorite scenes are
where I retreat into my quiet
skinning mangoes, their oozing
ripeness sucked bare to bone, we
then stupored on verandas beneath
the night's necklace of glow-worms

My favorite scenes are
where Enid Blyton's, picnics
seduced me to glazed places
of make-believe, moist cakes
school-work and expectation
to be home well before dark

My favorite scenes are
where decades are packed in
boxes of unbridled tchotchke
gathered cobwebs from cities
we left behind, each a woven
abode to corpses of my exiles

My favorite scenes are
where herbs are laid out
on newspaper sheets, basil
mint, coriander, parsley, I
savor their aroma, separating
tender leaves from stalk —

bartering each colander of greens
for another ghost story from the
bottom of her cauldron of
haunted things

"heart, liver, kidney" she whispered
dadi's repertoire of ghost tales was
e n d l e s s like
　　　　　her e n d l e s s
　　　　　　　　　　brows

In my Nani's house, curds and whey were a religion

Rendered warm
the milk in homage to perfect temperature
every drop just enough
dripping a muted prayer on nani's wrist.
Stately it would reside on the dining table
in a glazed terracotta pot; its tenderness an immaculate gospel.

Spoonfuls smooth
like rays of moon.
An attentive healing
of my acidic chest.
Kindness revealed
after rested nights.

Persisting in pause and patience in my nani's house.
Sallow in its maturing, whisked tidily into incubation.
The ritual of curd-making harnessed my attention
for precision and process, for transformation.
An unveiling of the delectable aphrodisiac
on alabaster mornings, always a ceremony.

I have failed to assemble curd like that, mine
settles in watery mouthfuls of regret.
It tastes hollow like
an afterthought, forgetting
to tighten its surface muscles
it collects into itself
refusing to be real
curd, metamorphized.

I have tried so much to do what Nani did but the
curd I make always looks like half fulfilled wishes.
As if it is telling me to have more patience, wants
me to breathe in, breathe out and stir the silence.
   The chewy curd I assemble
   is reluctant, uncondensed
   unlike the metabolic grace

in my nani's house.

Sometimes, I wish
    I had stood beside her more often
    watched her
    more closely.
    Her eyes an
    emblem of
    agni, akash
    an expanse
    in her arms.
    I wish I knew then
    that she was prithvi
    holding hostage an
    intoxication.
    I wish I had gathered stillness.
    I wish I had surrendered my
    questions to making of curd.

    There she is—
    looking at me sideways
    saree pallu sweeping to her waist
    a shining plait, pomegranate lips.

For the evil eye

memory tastes like a bitter gourd curry
the spiky taste insolent, just as sharp as
its skin, a rough and green exterior that
my grandma makes into a delicious dish
her hands scrape the obstinate bitterness
never hurried, she trims warts off the skin
with care, back and forth, back and forth
rubbing into it a carefully ground mixture
of spices —
three parts salt, one turmeric
a hint of cumin powder
one-part dry mango spice
her fingers crawling into and out of every
jagged corner of their snaky tenderness
stubborn yet subdued as one by one they
are packed and dropped into a bowl —
my day is astringent, an overstuffed aroma
starts to inhabit my palette in preparation
as she continues to de-fang their juices
salting each melon with an assurance as
her eyes find untamed twine, seamstress
style she fixes them into firm knots
her knuckles tying into
these knots our stories
confided, told, untold
all along humming a prayer, suffused with
a nectarine sweetness of words I do not so
understand, yet they make their way into me
my cyan core, its peskiness scooped out, and
gives way to her songs. Every word is tossed
as it finds a firm hold; like those peppercorns

she very carefully places inside the centered
womb of the bitter gourd parcels—
          "for the evil eye" she says
elegantly dropping her parcels
one by one
into an iron skillet, in scorching oil they
flicker
erupting
slowly salvaging
into their furrowed ridges her prayers, and
the amorphous kasturi of the shifting sun
finally, the pith is preserved in oval jars
brimming with a bouquet of aftertastes.

Hourglass

I hold solitude
in my hourglass
it falls in mineral grains, certain like
the fire that blew tongues of time
through the neck of the vessel
every second rains into
shadows of hope
in a free fall of
swooning
whispers, it
pierces into
an opal absence
an exaggerated silence
the stubborn quartz particles
in my hourglass are solitude, they
surrender together, yet disparate
still eroding by habit
grain by grain

Nanapapa

Nanapapa was a voracious reader

Readers Digests, Huckleberry Finn, Britannica encyclopedia
Great Gatsby
all the Agatha Christie series
Sydney Sheldon
Jane Austen
Collected Shakespeare
Keats
Rudyard Kipling
Khushwant Singh
Of course, Charles Dickens
The Old Man and the Sea
Shining copies of Misha and Soviet Union stacked together
An unabashed Quran too

then he grew older, his wife, my nani passed away
and aloneness arrived in abundance
an awkward reader now, voracious

Nana still remained
a voracious reader
perennially marking
the edges of pages
sometimes signing
his name, often he
left them open too

Nana retreated for hours
into his chair, still holding
her scent in its cushioned
shadows. He dusted each
book and saved it inside
a walnut chest, then kept
an empty perfume bottle.

Now a lender, from a reader
his mahogany walled library

became a display of video cassettes
I remember, the alchemy of that room

emblazoned by a vision, an addiction
dotted with names of movies, lettered

spines ascending floor to ceiling
white jackets, with black borders

handwritten names, meticulously
aseptic, I would sit cross legged

not in a padmasana, in that room
each rowdy summer as it gathered

an entire brood of cousins binging
on mangos scooped into eating contests

drowned with a spicy ambrosia of
buttermilk, our veins now drunk

laying claim to vanilla ice cream
shaped like the bricks of Augustus

that summer afternoon, after him
I stole four VHS cassettes, signed

also entitled myself, to his de luxe
gramophone & a rattan rocking chair

they say that the lifespan
of a video tape is 25 years
then pixilation sets in

Orb – for Kabir's parents

first poem
my buoyant fetus
sucks his thumb

swelling earth
a butterfly fluttering
inside

careful spring
my hands follow
your webbed toes

furtive sky
your pondering form
quietly warm

gibbous moon
the mirror reflects
a swollen belly

aperture
her eyes a window
to the unborn soul

recognition
kicking in the dark
to your name

reality check
the baby will emerge
unclenched

due dates
he offers the gift
of waiting

papa
your chest cradles
my shriveled skin

For Kabir

I want to leave you hummingbirds
meticulously feathered in pollen of
birdbaths, levitating conspicuously
into liminal spaces, perseverance in
stamina and speed, humming along.

> I want to leave you the history lesson
> your great grandpa wanted to write
> the story of his father, Sardar Saheb
> he was called "brave like a lion" and
> had a voice that rumbled like oceans.

I want to leave you the distance of
home, the one your father wishes
for with his breath and body, ever
standing at the fountain of missed
coins, offered to their tangled tales
the reluctance of my accented verse.

> I want to leave you hymns, chanted
> unspooled, memory of His rhythms
> shared as lullaby, so enchanting its
> sounds, it seeps you in nectar of a
> quivering voice, you close your eyes
> into lacquered sleep, hummed quiet.

I want to leave you with
every dawn and dusk of
my life stitched in prayer.

Decoding

My father and I
beneath the monarch oak
a sapling thrives

treasure hunt
eighty-five years of
fortitude

anchor
your voice guides
me home

Eleven Photographs in my Ma's Kitchen

One
I am a stirred kitchen pot of bubbles
a melancholy rehearsal on repeat
Two
I am a microcosm of brimming smells
of spices, flavors and fish scales
Three
I am an alchemy of meter and rhyme
of rum with chocolate marzipan
Four
I am a pitcher of iced sherbet
a keeper of sticky memories
Five
I am a bowl of orange pips, lemon
an explosion of cosmos in pitchers
Six
I am a page of sonnets between water sips
mouth overflowing with condensed tastes
Seven
I am a bowl of luscious terracotta caramel
of a delicate voice melting into burnt edges
Eight
I am an avalanche of muddy fudge squares
Of perennial answers to unspoken questions
Nine
I am an earthen platter of pickled sunshine
a crisp bite supplementing all prosaic days
Ten
I am a texture of overcast ginger and garlic
of unspoken appetites for buoyant curries
Eleven
I am an endless anthology of preserved scars
a testament to the hallowed spaces of silence

The Kitchen that is also a Monastery

I wish to memorialize the
kitchen in your home, one
where you meditate at the
stove, a nameless penance.

each pancake a gospel
for which we
saved powdered
sugar from a red tin jar
that deliberated, monk like
alone on your kitchen shelf.

Your kitchen is also of abundance
It watches over the content manner
of your chopping, saintly—
measured cubes of
squeaky clean vegetables
sharp by cut, layered
onions first, pink blushed
potato squared, then
dropped into a bowl
of ice-cold water
a slow devotional
playing on repeat
your eyes melting into tears.
carrots and peppers
always in juliennes
cauliflower florets
perfectly pristine as
you flicked them apart.
I remember watching
in awe, your fingers
elegant as they threw
shadows on egg white
walls.

Your kitchen is also a monastery
I remember you humming
a symmetrical prayer
with a quick move of your
wrist, you submerged sparse
offerings into a fiercely clean
pan—
one that sputtered spotless
as it gathered your warmth
meanwhile, you stirred life
into us, our faces cupped
in the folds of your
turmeric stained
hands –
held by a firm wrist
draped in a beaded rosary.

Your kitchen is so radiant
I remember you as
stubbornly insistent
about the dailiness of
ardaas/arzdasht
for sarbat da bhala
as you were about the
exact proportions in
those healing spoons of
five
spice –
I remember the kitchen epoxy
being bathed in a dewy caress
a periwinkle blue-purple gaze
of heavens stopping by dawn.

In the image of my mother

I can bask in the sunshine of
of watching my mother halt
her day—
> after she was done carving
> meaning into our lives
> as she etched our days
> with syntax
> of lunch boxes
> with storytelling
> under whirring fans
> with petulant warmth
> of a fresh casserole
> with newly learned
> dessert platters, sweet
> with nights offered on
> her lap, birth scents
> with lessons crafted
> from filigree of aches
> with mystery found
> in garnet drops, shapely
> with clicking tic tac
> of long knitting needles
> with bookshelves
> encased in first words

I remember relishing moments
of crying into her diaphragm
listening—
> her voice a clasp around our lives
> her hair swirled in a prosaic bun
> shaped like a cloud, introspecting
> she came alive, play-acting scenes
> from those famous silent movies

I half remember swallowing her voice
sashaying into our eager senses as
it hummed, sang, scolded or stayed
just stayed. silently.

I indulge, in remnants of her image
palpable, the pot leaps and boils
rebuking me, carelessly
I roll up my hair into a
rare bun, a nacreous wave
her syllables inhabiting me
from an unnamed distance.

Love Poem for all my Women

She spoke through her handiwork of
crocheted moments, stitching distances.

She comforted ghosts of growing arcs
fears gathered into her paisley shawls.

She tasted for us, in small bites which
her fingers broke into unaware mouths.

She wove pearls, starlight into blankets
that covered our fevers, craved warmth.

She held our whispers inside the silent
sun and lulled them to sleep in a hush.

She tidied our glances, and our mess
in unison with her tiptoed manners.

She adequately measured moondust
in ample spoonfuls of unlikely herbs.

She embellished marooned memories
a feather stitch piercing into their hems

She made the night listen, to chorus
of infinite conversations between us

She claimed our faults like they were
hers, painting them into silk scarves.

She grew our habits in precise ways
trimming rough edges, as of hedges.

She journaled in a cursive so curiously
alive on a page, making constellations.

She became Shiva, and his consort too
if needed she would awaken a tandav.

She practiced mindfulness of single
words, collecting shukr shukr shukr.

She is my equinox, balance brimming
with all seasons, I hold my axis in her.

Assemblage

Polishing the brass frame that houses my father's medals.
I assemble pieces and parts for the making of a man.
Serrated sunlight hits the medallions, squinting my eyes.

I run my finger over every oval bronze
a silver too, a badge, some pins - atoms
I linger at their fraying ribbons of blue silk.
Fragments of a stippled past, his history in
these nuggets.

I take stock. I count. I wait.
Adding, dividing
subtracting.
Repeat.

Total bars on the medal bar.
How many medallions within
the trembling oxidised frame?

Total number of years my father
had diligently pinned the badge
to his lapel.
The sum of collar pins divided
by the total number of cities.
He had seen iterative full moons
that had extended their arms to
his cities, welcoming.
I walk towards
the dinner jacket.
I dust it. Straighten the shoulders.

Portals

Doorways that summon us, then reveal of and to us

Windows and Rooms

The windows of all my lived houses
are bordered in conversations
and accents that lead to more rooms.

Like whispers, movements within the
solemn air, a sharp snake hissing into
stretched crevices.
The doors of these houses become
dancing altars that keep ghosts outside.
Like termite that eats into edges
unfinished stories crawl into the floors.

I walk barefoot across an empty courtyard
towards a kaleidoscope of cities, and secrets.
These cities emerge one by one from every
unused corner between rooms. Each city a
breath, transcreated into memories. Each
memory shuffling through unborn time.
They stay.

I move through each city, treading on its
sidewalks and letting its roofed shadow
move with me.
Disappearing.

I gather corners of cities
into the fragile folds of my
own gravity, creating homes.
t
e
t
h
e
r
e
d
to the stillness of bones
my marrow thrashing

against all the nights lost
inside sleep's charcoal flesh.

I decorate a curved alcove
with the sprayed sediments
of my own body.

Portrait of a mother in America

You are an unstoppable maverick
        you tenderly define the fossils we shall be
You are restless as you lie awake
        your forgiveness is now a lung emptied of breath
You are monastic as you listen to the bells ring
        your joy transient in yet another uncounted night
You are a widow wailing at the steps of a lake
        a practiced palanquin bearer of skinned surrender
You are a witch with long arms
        they embrace bodies showered from dilating skies
You are songwriter, fact narrator
        watchwords are written in your inherited ink
You are awake, you awaken, teasing
        your dreadlocks into witness stands, for the dead
You are yesterday's battles and tomorrow's cries
        you beat in ballads, rehearse poems to throbbing drums
You are louder with each breath
        penetrate a deafening normal, inside and outside
You are repetition, you sketch a scrawl
        that leaves scars on a country's cardboard map
You are hunger, your sharp tongue bites into cornbread
        ready again for another funeral pageantry
You are unabashed, you offer your breast
        to beating chests, fostering care for conjugated loss
You are ricocheted through our mistakes
        your prayer is a pause inside vacant throats
You are conversation to our silence
        you pour questions into our coagulated eyes
You are a mosaic of common journey
        your pilgrimage is to places where multitudes died
You are sister, you are princess
        you dance in compassion, holding your head high
You are your ancestors, you are healer
        you make garments of their velvet flagellated skins

You are language, farmer of roots
       you nourish the irreverence of all marching youth
You are baptized, you are ostracized
       you drink from the thirsty fountain of wakeful lives
You are time, of all moonless times
       you rudder the sea to the sky, you swallow meteorites
You are inadequate in your koans
       you ache in psalms that sing into life and afterlife
You are relentless, a stitcher of quilts
       you fill it with absence, thread it with sinew of barren wombs

A Woman folding laundry

piles stacked exactly in corners, an installation
of cropped joggers and fading t-shirts, a hoody
her limbs spurred out of inertia become wings
that flap into textures of each garment, folded
like clouds, lifted wide as if she were a feathered
bird in mid-flight. the fragrance of a washed load
envelops her body with a language of sameness—

unruly insistence of shirts, linen, tablecloths, etc.
the same sprays of sweetness, a citrus fragrance
permeating her wicker baskets, she exhales into
distances, she lifts up slivers of sleep from inside
an embroidered pillowcase, two roosters in red
so radiant, alive against the white of a bone dry
bedsheet. the scent of velvet skin dust of babies
that had stubbornly stayed inside moss stitch
squares of pastel knitted blankets. coffee kisses
persistent like unhealed wounds. tea stains of
maps on kitchen napkins, each absent inside
gingham checks. then the rare silk scarf, moist
in its paisley printed colors. a lush reminder of
mango-season, she keeps it clean and breath
fresh, ready to submerge into its abundance.
like a pirate's pockets, she too finds treasures.
perfectly washed trousers have pockets that are
lined with kerchiefs, taffeta crocheted into lace
with scalloped edges like moonlight falling into
the rapture of a waiting riverbed, its loneliness.
handkerchiefs that are awkward like shadows
scurrying shapes, some crumpled, one crushed
with the weight of unkept promises, some neat
observers to a bad day, starched white and tight
one presses itself to the face of just another day.
She folds them into dainty squares, her crackling
fingers running along the edges of broken hems,
absentmindedly

she
refolds the folds
corner to corner
wipes her blank
salty face, pleats
held in place—

she gathers her perennial
hair, wandering into the
waiting arms of laundry
          she lifts up a stark
          white shirt, waiting
inside the wet alchemy
of another bucket load.

So much yet to be said
So much still not heard

Parents

they made me
sinew and flesh
and mind
they still stay
        an incense
        alliterative
as if to
remind me, in
its lifelong scent
that I will make
my children who
they become, and
so, this curse will
never leave me of
being the parent
and seeing them
in the gaze of my
clouded mirror, I
let them stay
        their presence
        my minotaur
steeped like pain
inside my blood
invisible like the
dissipating mists
lingering outside
their presence is
persistent, blister
in my mouth, a
constant twitch.

in honor, I repeat
the rituals of being
parent, I insist on
doing what they
did for me, I pray.

I exorcise prayers of
homebound tongues.
I persist in fragments
of their staccato songs.
I practice measured
mantras, rise and fall.
I insist on inheriting
the legacy of their loss.

Ordinary Love

masked smiles
love catches itself
in crinkled eyes

this birthday
a disinfected bouquet
of wood roses

an argument
a lavender poultice
under my pillow

our names
tattooed on my back
a leaking roof

touching palms
on facetime calls
showing up

ode to joy
celebrating life
across balconies

heritage walk
finding love stories
in ink and stone

Meditations on Egg

Mary Oliver – "When it's over, I want to say all my life I was a bride married to amazement"

The moment when I stand in the middle
of the kitchen and wonder how an egg
would describe fullness—
Tending itself with a shell
Fragile neat oval
A deliberate embrace, its heart swimming
        inside a goblet, albumens pondering
around the pearlescence of the glazed yolk
        present with a purpose, its nourishment
integral yet undiminished from the whole
        a moment of fullness in the way it rests
on its edge, a planet on her orbit, whispering
into its own curves
The narrow end
        balancing the other
        in keen care, carrying
pushing towards the heart, ovum in its care
in exactitude, bound in membranes
Of chalazae strings
        till it is cracked
        un umbilicus
        un moored
into chaos, liqueur —
        shell, sponge, liquid
        emerges, reborn
        into a lagoon
        grows outward
        a lake, flatness now
        peppered with salt

My balance, finding
Point Nemo, the eye
of every empty circle
every moment
is full, pregnant
until it is not

Becoming Planets
After Greta Thunberg

If I could be a planet
I would like to be Mercury
baring myself to the sun, those times
when I need brightness seven times stronger than myself

Or maybe the clumsy Uranus
Stuttering sideways, self-effacing but
Living the moods of my 27 moons and
Never having to explain myself before or after menopause

I have even speculated about Mars
Red in the face, evidence of my travails
Receding further into my atmosphere, I would
Mock the men who stumbled for oxygen, after kissing me

Maybe Neptune is who I will be
Distant, forlorn and cold to touch
Icicles inside my craters, as I paced
Centuries of blackholes, no one to fault my goddess

I am a planet though; as every woman before
I bleed myself hollow; I swallow my volcanoes
I spin for all before me who were dwarfed
I draw orbits around names of all our departed souls
I weave a Kuiper belt with the fallen ringlets of my hair
I gather our screams till they pierce through veins of these stars
I repeat all of the above, I rotate, I revolve, I burn, I am born
into the firmament above—

I become my solar system, my tears crystallize into
brooding planets, swaying to the *blah blah blah* of
a flawed Earth as it still manages to trudge along

How a Woman delivers Hope

She embroiders the tundra with her hushed moans, breathless
As a tightness tugs and untugs within her, hesitating, punctuating
She watches the air meet flesh at the outline of her being
As calm unsettles into rivulets flowing from inside of her
She pushes into beginnings, and rises into endings—

>   still
>   patient
>   warrior
>   woman
>   giving
>   birth

As the universe rises in *thumri*, swirling slogans into light
She follows other women, their flaming, screaming, breathing
As her urging sinew and muscle shift, pulsing her towards life
she renews herself with a sumptuous feast of goddess light
As it ebbs and flows, unfurling grit, reciting the new
reciting the new, reciting the new as the midwife guides
she oozes eternity into the space between her thighs, rising
into a crescendo, the protests outside grow vacant with cries
she enunciates freedom for her body, and offers an exile to that
which was held within hers, pushing, brimming, pushing, bearing
delivering hope into a pregnant pause
And a glistening head now emerges—

Into the hands of her convulsing grace
Into fragility of a land that walks barefoot
Into earth men that peddle her to goddesses
Into monuments that stand on quick sands
Into rivers sterile for they are bleeding dry
Into flags that flutter with septic infusions
Into stuttering prayers of a laboring country

How a woman leaves behind
drenched stories, sputtering
from the stone of her wasted
wombs – she delivers enough
drenched, wet, unfolding hope.

Green Tea is only a Placebo

Awakened to a half-finished poem. Detailed. Placid.
I slip back into sleep. Buddha like. Trance. Meditative
I write. About letting my thickening body find respite
from its own environmental disruptions. A slave and
master of its changes. Unpredictable as it clutches at
love and hate – both extreme like the walled feelings
of Troy —
laying into each hopscotch square
my peri menopausal events—
enraged like the fortune of Hecuba, hushed.

unexplained migraines impact my pupils' tolerance
to light, the dark soil of my brain being scooped out
like the innards of a thanksgiving turkey, its cartilage
wound into knots, fissures lined with a rumbling ache.

a bruised broccoli buttock is now real, I tuck them in
squeezing tight, wondering what I would write for my
funeral instructions. I gather my daily pauses in ellipses
Each ellipse holding a vibration in its Trojan belly.

I invest in shunya
it comes in handy—
allows me to get small talk right during cyclical
gynae visits
allows me to respond to vinegary questions posed
by her
my organic-shampoo-keepsake-hair-type doctor
in birkenstock's
she is so perfect; it is nauseating
but her google reviews
average at 5 and so, I
enroll with her again this year.

My daughter says research and reviews
are important, I read 7 of them spread
evenly between good, bad
and indifferent.

Moreover, Dr. Shimbley always has open appointments
on weekends. On other days, I have to deal with a job.

hair on my chin is showing up
uncontrolled like falling meteors
ornamenting my face, emptiness
in rhetorical questions, like those
in a New Yorker school poem.

My nocturnal hibernation is
ever full of a mundane noise
as the architecture of temples
hovers over gathered pilgrims
it is a marvel if I don't snore
like a whirlpool, drifting in a
never ending circle, inwards.

My days are filled with constant vasomotor
chatter of 'It is so hot' or 'It is so cold' or
'It is all because of you'. avoid alcohol they
say, but green tea is only a placebo. I think
finishing a poem is a better idea, deliberate
about my sentences, the shorter the better.

Meanwhile, you have been sleeping in the guest bedroom
often these days, you need to be well rested for a new day
even God gets tired, and you my dear, are just a human.

I mark my notebook for the next appointment
my knees will be tapped and tested, empty of
any cushioning, just human knees walking into
the future, creaking.
Slowly but surely, I will be master
of decadence, palpitations. Initiated.

Even Troy is an investigation to unrelenting time.

Happiness – refrigerator magnets

I.
My dad loves a perfect sunny side up. I look out of the window at the trees from the house I am in. I am isolated and sustaining kindness in myself by making perfect sunny side up eggs everyday. I make two of them today. Somedays, I taste acerbic memory in my mouth. Other days, I dissect the sun of its glow and hold it by the pale rim. It bleeds into my heart like the ochre yellow of a runny spoonable yolk. I wonder how genetic codes untangle from each other to make us who we are. I murmur to myself as I heat the pan. Just like my mom. I am no longer impatient with my husband for wanting them cooked in exact circles.

II.
My mom always gathers random flowers on her walks. She watched over her garden like a hawk. Her home always so proud with vases tucked away in every corner, filled with bullrushes, and zinnias, sweet peas and wildflowers. I gather this moment as if it may not be here tomorrow. I capture it both on my phone and inside of me. With my fingers I touch the flowers as if they are watching me like my mother had watched over me as a child, being both my wish and my prayer. Like her flower arrangements, they nod absentmindedly, almost habitually as if dusting off their own pollen. It is dusk. I look away before the blue of the sky starts to sear and insist on settling into my eyes. My aqueous humor always at the edge of dripping like the water in mom's ikebana vases. I hustle towards the railroad. I like balancing on the railway tracks and hearing her say, your spine should always be an upright stalk, girl. I harvest her voice, and press the flowers.

III.
My children are just a phone call away. We talk about things to do and things we have done. They take me through their lives. Like a garage sale, I look around curiously at their knick and knacks wondering which one I can bring away at a bargain price and they would not even notice. Outside, it is all normal like a scene from a train window - the blooming sky, the nip in the air, the trees turning pale, a scurrying scavenger, the large sky. It is not until I look at the neatly assembled family of ducks striding along the lake that I begin to cry. I trust the lyric of the forlorn bird that sings to river waves. In the same way I

would hum an ordinariness to them, when my children were young and still liked lullabies and warm milk. I listen to the *queg-queg-que* of the magpie and hear myself falling through the quiet grooves of her song.

IV.

My life just like all of ours is now a stillness. Still in the same place. Still deep and shallow, still. Droning alongside, time is leaving behind messages of being fine. It rings in the day and brings in the night. Teaching us to be thankful we are alive, and learning the uses of hydroxychloroquine. The sun still rises and scenes still get created, recreated with babies and dogs on walks, with parents wearing N-95 masks. It is okay or will be soon, and everyone thinks it is charming to be alive, still. I write a few more uncomfortable poems for another pandemic anthology. It is humbling that editors are still reading about time and tide. Words still set themselves at the table each daybreak.

Hushed Snow

glassy music
silence scattering
across snow

arched doorway
a rainbow bruises
the sky

future
tea leaves tremble
in my cup

rinsed sky
your presence lingers
in scents

equality
shimmering white
of winter

carved message
on melting snow
farewell

our fireplace
familiar hands
feel cold

Aubade

when you are a father
watch for the arriving dawn
it will bring a chirping swallow
that has tended to its new born
watch it lift itself, sure and strong
nest settling below your windowsill
her beak holding dilated beams of light
just one chirp so enough to create music
of a hidden earth, sky, diaphragm of souls
the swallow flies to and fro, beating retreat
she settles on unsettled ground, moving all
along towards nested cries, and stilled waters
much gathered in her abandonment to warmth
when you are father, your nights will so awaken
as mornings rouge your face with a tender sleep

When you are a father, drink in translucence
When you are a father, marvel at baby echoes
When you are a father, hold life in your palm
When you are a father, collect ripples of tears
When you are a father, lean into his breathing
When you are a father, paint tiny fingerprints
When you are a father, unbecome your father

The Birthing Scenes of Charles River

Imagine the sight of a river
perpetual outside your window
I allow myself to find my window
and swallow the sights that hang in
hunched lifetimes, from a stilled sky.

Thrusting itself out of calloused dawn
the bosom of its crumpled wet pleats
is as tender as the bursting breasts of
a new mother. Its urging nectar flows
towards a keen south, stretched long.

Imagine that a season is also
pushing its way out of a ripened
vagina, amniotic waters ready for
it to emerge. A season finding its
crescendo in rustling sounds as it
shrugs away the grey of weariness
and dips into the courtyard of the
velveteen waters, the bird sounds
an orchestra to a crowning wonder.

I notice how the maples form
a nursing dome, keeping watch.

I also keep watch, on
vigil at my window
as an umbilicus uncoils
over oblivious stones
      Farther away, Eliot's fog
      is carefully forgetting the
symposium of mountain peaks.

I still the waters within myself
toss my coins out of the window
into the fountainless labyrinth. I
squint as I stare at the stark light.

Waiting

how you swallow yourself

when asleep
and I watch you my love
my gaze ripens as I hear
your breathing into
the quiet of my heartbeat
it listens to the universe
humming—
to crickets singing aloud
without a care
to the creaking windows
to the obscene winds
to the owls throating
I smell the pungent
silence as the boughs
bend to kiss the leaves
with the defiance of just
revealed green
I watch a worm crawling
into forest of grass blades
making love to a curdled earth

I watch, have watched you
for many such visceral nights
I wish for my gaze to ripen
into the shape of your bones
I watch, and hush
my churning veins
I continue sketching our names
into the keen of your curled back
clefting fleetingly
into the carousel
of our silence

waiting inside unfinished stories, is the
punctuation of any extra ordinary love.

Dear Husband

watching the precise breaths
that you offer each night when
we turn into the cellophaned
ends of
our nights.

as light creeps through doors
ajar, rooting into our quenched
bodies, I grow into your breath
a predator.

as the morning is embalmed in
the warmth of your voice, songs
stay captive in the flirting of our
shared contemplation.

watching the precise breaths
that you offer each night is the
exact reason I exist,

scribbling into each
inhale and exhale
anchored.

our white noise
repeating itself
uninterrupted.

Pagri
Turbans

All my writing was born into
the folds of my father's pagri
one in each fold of his khaki—
cotton, starched, smooth, sturdy
I attempted to shape stanzas with
my tongue, while my hands pulled,
stretched, unbound all the 6 yards
of cloth, unfurling beginnings
—

I proudly held at one end on
mornings when I was called
upon to help twist the length
the landscape of that moment
had a spirituality, a gravitas, it
snatched at my throat, settling
into creased circles, my voice
had so much to say, instead in
quiet observation I gave it all
my care, all my curiosity—
His prayer had a very specific
tempo, I never dared disturb it
I saw an intimate conversation
sprouting into the empty spaces
of teacher and disciple, unsaid.
A sacred hum became audible
I heard stories being revealed
as elders sang hymns in waves
gentle metaphors were formed
in faith as a circular wrapping
folded and unfolded words, they
became mine, unborn into me as
I held the fabric taut, was taught
letters, my fingers at the edge
of a long pagri he so reticently
pulled at the other, tugging just
so, he said to me each time we
symmetrically styled a turban

in performance together —
"you, my daughter, my poem"

Pagri–

Pagri, and its different transliterated variations is the term for turban worn by different communities in the Indian subcontinent. It specifically refers to a headdress that is worn by men and women, which needs to be manually tied. In this particular poem, the reference is to the turban worn by Sikh men and the ritual of tying, wearing and pride associated with the pagri. As the years evolve the pagri becomes a metaphor for many complex cultural and familial intersections that the poet has experienced and associates with this word and its rituals – both the physical act of tying, the bonding with a father and the symbol of strength, empowerment, creativity and spiritual grounding this word and its image has offered the speaker and others like her.

Functions of a Saree

1.

I always tried to get their shade right, the commemorative fuchsias a disaster spilling sky waiting to break open. Matching a choli, its strings as important as a seatbelt in a new car. The giddy 9 yards surrounding my curves, neither the naughty bandhani nor my spilling body knowing when to flow in a straight line. Like a river it climbed over waiting stones, touching unspoken talismans of places that existed before being found, rummaging through my veins. Its caress visited the creaks and crevices of my ruffled geography, depositing strange feelings. Together our anatomy unwieldy.

2.

Later, like birds forming into poems, I walked with a spring in my step, each chamber of my heart beating with the precise colors of jeweled flowers. They swooned into the sarees my nani had left behind, neatly stacked in her locked closet. A mosaic weave, reflecting light like the stained glass in silent churches. Folded in a crisp brown bag, it sat in a stoic samadhi on reluctant shelves of her antique cupboard. Years of delicate attar lingered beneath the sarees, nani's unseen life becoming mine as I felt their niggling textures. Preening in front of the longing mirror, my cheeks pinched blushed, my eyes dripping with *kohl* canoes. Reminders of the woman tugging to exist inside the tightness of a petticoat. Her favorite turquoise *benarasi* embraced me, consuming me into itself as a lover ever would, as naked. Hypnotized.

3.

These days when I undrape my saree, I creep back into my body, my ample darkness a snake moving backwards, climbing into its own metallic skin, untangling it from the aftermath of a perforated monsoon creek. My determined flesh refuses to be curtained into perfect shapeliness. It stays, stubborn like the crumpled *pallu* of a muslin *jamdani*. The black and lilac embellished satin saree nani wore on her last birthday hangs lopsided, an unmended pendant waiting to be worn.

4.

Soon, I will wait behind that paisley *jamdani* saree as it animates my window, the oceanic gauze of its warp and weft will sieve light into the shimmering map of my hypnotized body. It will stay unaffected. Meanwhile, I will invoke the rubble of scars beneath an untarnished *kanjeevaram,* letting them bleed into the luster of its lissome gold borders.

silkworm spins
itself into a grave -
kanjeevaram

An Ode to Paused Cities

A paused spring
in convalescence
A pandemic sings
of equivalence
A people paused
as battles rage

A critical loss
of life in triage
A busy morgue
of consequence
A distance locked
yet defenseless

Dormant Rituals

after Amanda Gorman

when the world
is better, less bitter
we will inherit again
migrate again
settle,
unsettle again

we will stand
tall, look each
other
in the eye,
non posturing,
          again
we will be
          free
in our language
again, phrases
poetry, words
not sanctified
expressions
we will begin
again, with
pride
our shoulders
in hope
will steer us
there
again
we will migrate
and unmigrate
          again

what is
done
again
and
again
is   ritual
is   practice
near   perfect
things like
dressing the
dead, smiling
through
missing
teeth,
dodging
bullets in
alleys
of grocery
stores
cracking eggs
in equal halves
hiding stains
of
menstruation,
spilling guts
neatly inside
paper bags.

we will migrate
and unmigrate
again
existing
without insult

the ritual
of being
dormant
will soon
light our hearts
with fluorescence
a desire to belong
to the hill beyond
the one we could
not climb.

Love in the Foyer

The shimmering
zest of your skin
rubs into my clay
like a secret sin, I
am an oblique glance
towards the kindred
sun, liquid as it slips
into the erupting sea.

my mornings
awaken to
the light
your ocean's
wildness
drop by
drop by
drop
flapping/pulsating/learning.

carefully
my pores
marinate into the
molecules of your
luscious color
your rainbow
gathers my rage
mends its curling
ripe skin, touching
my cocoon on the
inner side, you be
                come a monarch
                lurking inside my
                chrysalis—
waiting
to be stripped of
a preserved death.

our translucent eyes
become an altar-piece
of plenitude, gushing
in slow-motion, a fall
of confetti, gathering
a petulant amorphous
silence.
in sangam.

          each wisp of our breath
          opens its mouth towards
          a trembling
          echo of us
          time hangs upside down
          as our wings exclaim in
          exquisite desire, in the
          hemolymph' ed foyer
          of our ~~unpresent~~
          afternoons.

All in a Day, in 2020

~~Surrender~~

when serrated sunlight filters
into my eyes each morning
I scrub myself clean, unbraid
the decayed night and
walk out into symmetrical days

when the letterbox opens
to sanitized envelopes
of latticed anger, stamped
with squares of waxed death
I kneel within the center

of my erased garden, lisping
a series of crumpled words
God, Oh God, Please God
while the sky starts to erupt
in thunder naming all lives

no longer glowing, in flesh
of fermented fevers.
I see angels' hover

~~unmasked~~

they straddle my screams
on the sheer of their wings

as I tug at the remaining
sprouts of grass, trembling
my veins sink into a still
patient earth, while
a volcano rages in
her riddled graves

in that moment
my bruised
breast beats
for the gods
awaiting its
last breath

Empathy

Because in between the crisp morning of my bedsheets
I wonder why confinement feels so uneven and on edge
is it
because one is exposed in barrenness to those who share
our space, the blood-streaked skyline and its heaving waves
or is it
because one is forced inwards, watchful of rusting words
their sound hollow like the final whirring of resuscitation
or is it because
the tarantula is spreading its hips wider and wider into the
arched breathlessness of our tightening chests.

5,532,280 dead
Monday 17 January 2022.

Confession

Afterward, I weep into that mole
it waits, in shadows of your wrist
I smoothen it, lingering my teeth
in its near circle, filter coffee rust
I know its fissures too well by now
like a canoe on your melting skin
        I fetter to it, my anklets now mute.

Your Lotus Gaze

Your birthing is of unusual intervals
Your equanimity afloat on aftermaths
Your resistance rises in imperfections
Your voice is made of seasonless earth
You unpick whiteness
with your shadows

> make it blush with quietness of colors
> your petals close gently over each word
> each tongue a memory, bleeding azure
> into its veins. your birdsongs perch on
> upright spines, even as you wait inside
> pods of a thousand shimmering seeds
> each seed drowning into history, rising
> towards a vision of awkward blooming
> million lotus suns ready to be released

I urge her, this America, to receive, to
be absent enough to be vacant enough
to be still enough, to let her fault lines
show hurt enough, to be tall enough
to be Shyamala Gopalan enough, to be
innocent enough, to wear a crown made
with flowers, that are not flowers enough
to walk far, to walk deep into discomfort
enough, to change enough
to be upside down enough
to be capable of ovations
enough, open arms enough
to be America enough

to face square & fair
the frugal dawn of a moist lotus gaze
present between both water and earth

*For Vice President Kamala Harris wishing her presence and perspective of a lotus
on her journey.*

Limoncello Lotion

Winter, last year when I visited you.
you were settling into a new home.
"I feel more grounded there," I said
your nearness unrattles me, always"
anchored—
like the swaddling of a new born
like a nest of gathered warmth
like a time-capsule fused in calm

I threw my bags into the spare bedroom, the one
designated as mine with a knitted throw, like so
like so many I now possess, they travel with me
I have them in all shapes, sizes—
a multi colored spread with squares woven together
like the places and pieces of our lives, another one
knotted on its borders with jagged skeins of wool
a toasted brown. The dense colors of the blanket
permeated the room like your fragrance, infusing
the newness in the air with a burst of pecan tones.

You explained, you always do.
a step wise process. *"Here is the closet,"*
The keys to the almirah strung on
crocheted tassels, swaying reminders
of old habits. Swishing an onion pink
silk saree aside, you very
purposefully stated
"I've emptied it."

> *As if purging was even possible.*
> *You meant the closet.*

"and arranged your sarees on hangers.
Wear this one, a zephyr light pink
tussar for our lunch date tomorrow."
You wanted to ask me
about the thawing silver
in my hair, it matched
the silver of your antique
jewels. hesitantly oxidized.

You did not.

Instead, you offered direction, inane guidelines to
where the light switch was situated in the bathroom.
"left top corner of the wall to your right as soon as you enter"
the bookshelf lined with books
"old is gold" you said
pistachio colored paper
crisp like peanut skins.
arranged in zig zag pillars,
one on top of the other
just like the book lovers
posted on social media!
you had ensured towels
rolled tight as always
jasmine stalks in a tube
placed on the vanity
as always
this stem vase has held
tuberoses he sent for me
white, colorless, counted

You left the room, hurriedly
after a hesitant kiss on my
forehead.
as always.

I stood for a few minutes in front of the
closet, held a lace edged towel to my face.
I wiped my tears
"and when you cry, remember the source of the gift of all tears"
Joy Harjo's words reminded me that the source of
my tears was the fragility of nostalgia.
as always.

I picked a face cloth that had a bouquet
of pansies embroidered on each corner
and your lingering fragrance. lime. lemon.
permeated from your hands to our fingers
and minds. The lotion you have tenderly
rubbed into your hands, the citrus scents
now permanently sutured into your skin
a large jar of the cream, always waiting in
stoic resignation on your bedstand
another pump on the kitchen shelf.

I find a half-used limoncello lotion
bottle on the study table in my room.
I pump two bursts into my palms and
remind myself that this specific
fragrance has since been retired.
Now a vanished language of zest.
Memories.
Quarantined.

Detours

Alternate routes that deviate from the norm and help reshape our direction.

My Brother's dog Laika

for years I have
put its sound on a leash

Laika, your sparkling, slender
body
perfectly fitted into the
world.
Your nostrils quivered
in sleep, making others jealous
with how you got his attention
named so after the first mongrel
in space, Laika.

Laika, who joined the mission
to validate space
to prefix their story
while fulfilling a sad end
with a pounding heart.

you orbited him like
a prayer consistently
stable and kind.
he held you like
he was your earth.
your eyes
shimmering in sharp response
like darts to his deepening
sound —
Catch, he said
Go Catch
Laika

You were tonic to his youth
an unspoiled brat, like him
you too gazed into the eyes
of others with a sweetness
that crumbled their worlds.
I saw in you and him an

animated companionship
each time you gracefully
knocked at the door.
>   *racing*
>   *tumbling*
>   *folding*
>   *ears flapping*
nearly blind into his arms.
His days
glowed in your presence
your lives tucked into
each other
as if in knowledge
of what
was imminent
your pictures
bristle with friendship
simple moments
so expansive, you
staring at the camera
both breathless
it jolted me back —

It is raining today
I heard
you bark outside
lingering as you did
at the edge of his heels.
I nudge your scent away
Go, catch Laika, I say
It makes me want to ask though —

Are you both together, now?
Does he lean against you?

In his blue plaid shirt, his
cuffs unbuttoned
convenient
you at his side
quiet as you chew
so familiar, so present, so near
his hands reflexively
linger around your neck
ready for a quick walk.

Conversations

toothless,
my grandma prays
in another land
to be buried under
the lemon trees

here,
a solitary iris
bobbles its head
as I etch her name
on a memorial engraving

Just a process after all

"in our village are short and to the point." **Funerals by James Laughlin**

The hustle of the five days after you.
They prescribe 10 to 30 days of mourning.
The completion of mandatory actions like
curdled milk, ghee, oil lamps, candles, pristine sheets,
tilted tears, jasmine-filled condolences, food and guests.
Your hands placed in the position of prayer
as the floor was sprinkled with water.
Purification. Release. Rebirth.
Meanwhile, a forgotten notebook still open at your desk.
Your baritone voice barely gathered inside the cold walls of an urn.
Cannot bring ashes home or keep the urn in your room.
Ashes don't
germinate. life.
Ramification. Release. Rebirth.

I feel you. Almost grinning at the edge of the polished rim
before the brass vessel bobbles away into the setting sun.
The incense burns. Sandalwood.
Did you promise to reach me as soon as you arrive there?
We gather at the dinner table. Extended family and all.
Purgation. Release. Rebirth.
Today we serve rajma – chawal. Tomorrow is chicken curry day,
exactly like you relish it. Marinated overnight. Well washed. Clean.
I wish you could hear them asking me if I would write something
about the process of putting away life.
I wish you would come back. Turn around.
for a day. So, I could grab one soaked drop of your voice
                    and nest its vibration within my
                    rib-cage.
                    Salvation.

Miracles

sowing seeds
a departing squirrel
stiffens

tombstones
a cardinal circles
overhead

catharsis
every day I miss
your scent

new moon
scribbling again
on old letters

crickets chatter...
in typewriter sounds
I show up

Grief in a potli

breathing in the cold today
I felt your weight on my
eyelids.

a sullen sky yawns into its
horizon, stretching awake
as it stares at the robin
her eyes in gridlock with
the tinted regret of gods.
starlings meditate inside
murmurations, methodical
leaving behind a stilled tail
of coaxed departures.

I can hear the season turn
shadows fall in patterns of
immensities outside.

you
insisted on leaving behind
howls of open exit wounds
gathered into *potli's* of my
mother's erased smiles.

Desk Poems

crisp air
I wrap myself
in her shawl

breaking open
a sealed chest
of memories

fading music
holding her hand
a final time

basil tea
fragrance steeped
in last breaths

funeral home
the checklist includes
tulips

stillness
cicadas mourn
in chorus

Dendrochronology

Some questions start in the center of my belly, a soft hunger
others stumble out of my mouth, like acres of wild gardens
they fall from the sky, into the backyard of my night storms
stay like watchful steps of an elephant on my hunter's heart
I fill my breastbones with the fallen feathers from my porch
> with quills, I draw ripples over the river between us
> I conjure some answers and embroider each with a
> daisy stitch into the stretch circles that are emerging
> around my middle, each concentric ring now coded
> with questions and answers, like the stump of a tree.
> each code permanent as it keeps vigil on my ghosts.

Missing Questions

Some questions have been forgotten
I start to collect them as they lay invisible
within my body, scampering and whimpering
on foreheads, on spines, on breasts, in veins.

Some answers are to be found—
hiding in scorpion stings, that astound
victims into shock, or in corridors of darned skins
left behind by snakes as they ripple into newness.
in dew drops that filter the drizzling light of angels
or the aftertaste of death squatting in stagnant tears
perched on clouds shaped like our amused ancestors.

Begone

The bruised trees
called me awake today
I awakened
to their whipping voices
as they brushed, against
my skin
brimming over
the hummingbirds
whispering
rushed
towards honey bowls
their beaks colliding
spilling, I walked
slowly, surely, sorely
slowly, screamed—
my neck drawn taut
like those red breasted birds
for there was
fire
singing
a supple song
a fire that flamed
from embers of
last night—
of other nights
now in the past, yet
lingering like fugitive
bygones.
begone

I shouted
         begone now
you bruised trees
and you bristling voices
and untethered flowers
and colliding beaks
and forlorn forests

you
begone.

Cope

I hear
the shutters of my mind
opening to a fisherman's
song –
it is erupting
coughing
out of my body
all the
phlegm'ed dust, stripping
my fallowed skin
away from me and my
ever fiddling nerves.
I bend into my muffles
and hold my mandible
until there is no song.
To cope, my teeth are
forged into my jaws
anchored
like the calcified skull
of a fish, staring blind
into a rusted hook.

Normal

rare blue moon
another ambulance
and blue lights

obituaries
age, color, caste
no bar

tourist season
an empty colosseum
of silent coffins

war zones
a world-wide bunker
of chaos

shallow breaths
grandma whispers
a final blessing

cancelled flights
the godwit migrates
again this year

ocean waves
the dip and rise
of economics

Country

When did you stop listening to your own; become unwilling to look up
into our eyes;
look away from your own opiate limbs; look away from birthmarks on
your skin;
look away from the falling blisters of your eyes;
When did you become so lazy that you let the claws of your feet
burrow deep, trapped in your own blemished ground; unmoving even
when being eaten alive—

> by the blooming anguish of your people; by odors from
> floating carcasses of your soul;
> by the waves that beat against the sunken scales of your ghosts;
> by sordid drippings of
> pleas
> fleeing your own mouth.

At this very moment I am a lighthouse standing in watch; I am carving
my solitary light into ripples; each ripple a caterpillar pupating; a
butterfly pulsating to panchkritya of tandav dance; its wings flapping to
the spitting fire of a trillion monarchs; unwilling to diapause until you
listen to the whistling of their alliterative song.
They will circle you into an orchestrated garland, evacuating your
cauldron of prayers, and pledges, until you hear their buzzing silence;
they will drink incessantly of your matted milkweed, they will churn
intemperate until you hear anew.
For if you don't; an apocalypse is coming closer and closer towards
your shore; you have time now to gaze outwards and listen; to act
before being engulfed into the whirlpool of growling stillness; to
become the country we knew.

to become the country, we knew.

I Stopped Counting

oh ma
I am numb, a shadow
no matter how I hug my knees
I stay enclosed
since the day I swallowed
corpses of forced desires, startled silences
sometimes the clock forgets to chime
days dare to hurtle into nights, I
am drenched, palms down, flight ready
in a corner behind a dead door
the footsteps of each day, tense
and too loud
predatory
I sit wooden, still waiting
for the chariots of moonlight
sometimes ma
you forget about me
I feel you ma
you and your hustle bustle in the kitchen
gur with ghee, sizzling hot
your pallu tucked tightly at your waist
oh ma
that night
was their feast ma, that night
they were so many
many mouths
many hands
many men
many needs
secreting pheromones
as they came
one
two
three
four
five
six
seven

eight
nine
…………..
I stopped counting,
they masticated, animal and prey
my face, breast, thigh, neck,
orgy state of hunger, my finger
was hurting, ma
ma
I stopped counting at
nine, but there were many bilious men
uninterrupted butchers, they slept
and snored afterwards, sprawled
I bit myself, and my wounds
my bleeding tongue and ran
and ran
and ran
and ran
till I saw the bonfire
it was Lori[3], wasn't it ma
I love gur with ghee
      ma
        did you ever
        feel raped
as you lay outstretched
did you sometimes quiver
when he exited his manhood
satiated
grunting

I love gur with ghee
Sizzling hot on the surface
like
embers
on
a
pyre

Dear Daughter, and Son

I shrug my shoulders, I make another
square cardboard box. It takes forever
for me to perfect the steps of putting a
box together.

       One final time. I go through each closet
       in every room. In the house. No longer
       home.

       yours my daughter should be easy
       since you had said, *"Mama, you can
       give everything away. Just bag it to
       a donation or drop it outside the
       shelter home".*
I held a graduation gown, swishing
green in my arms. I stood a statue
your papa found me there, a heap
of levelled clothes next to me.

I have been staring a lot. empty.
hangers of shapes and sizes, limp
on rods inside vacant closets that
swallow the phrases caught inside
walls of this house. they gush into
the present. mutating.

       I am holding the box of key chains
       you collected as a boy, my dear son.
       of shapes, sizes, letters, city names
       they sat unremorseful in a rusted tin
       box. crowded. skeletal remains.
       "like a corsage of memories"

If I stood longer, even for a moment
I would come apart, disintegrate like
the oldness of this house, tear apart
like tissue paper, unwrapping muscle
of unnamed grief. I pack it quickly
into cartons. If I stayed, I would cry.

Instead, I pack boxes, with each box
I let go, pixelated shards. unnamed.
I know that some stranded pieces
will stay, stubborn like photo frames
that refuse to be undone from walls.
or leave gaping holes in the cement.
I find the tall Superman poster that is
wrapped in plastic sheaths stands tall.
It is perfect, unbearably present. then
there is the guest bedroom wall, one
that served as a height chart. earliest
marker shows you at 4 feet 5 inches.
how tall are you today?

I take a break every few hours
relabel the mislabeled boxes
accrue a few reminders, still
unfolding
shirts
unbuilding
puzzles.
I save
one ruby red nail paint
from your stack
for later. I don't
look up. look back.

                    unemotional
                    wearing your gingham
                    today

                    strokes
                    of frosted memories
                    another coat of red

Architecture of Death

      rooms after dead people
      leave
are like wells
an aroma of velvet lichen
that glisten over narrow
curves of its walls
the water within
stagnant, brackish, mute

      rooms after dead people
      leave
are like wells
people peering inside
the bodice of its edge
their shadows blooming
weeping willows resting
against embalmed edges

Chittarkatha - last night with her at the care ward

I have it down to a science
but they say it is an art too
I have been shaping
mantras
from my lips to yours
my eyes are waterfalls
they travel unfettered
that night, I brought
your favorite books along
you preferred silence, your
fingers encasing my spine
they knew each vertebra, its code
I wipe you down, cooling your fever
reminding you about
your tinctured tongue– sharp and electric
how my words
have spent centuries
inside your spinal fluid
syllable
by syllable
embedding
looped stories from
my atlas to your axis

I grasp at your iris, the fish floating
inside them, they mist over
for one last time, as if to sip
at the full bellied cry
that is rising in me,
your pulse gripping my fingertips
as I listen to your errant beating
at Erb's point—
        lub dub
        lub dub
        lub dub
        lub
        lub
        lu
        l
        l
        ...
fading punctuations
a dancing wind chime
I cover your absent face
with one porous poem
the final one, an obituary
written by your bedside
I let it unfurl, like a new born leaf
it bleeds a hibiscus into your veins
they calcify, I braid your bare hair

        meanwhile, the nurses
        get ready with a checklist

Chitrakatha - *chitra* meaning picture and *katha* meaning story.
Chitrakatha is the Indian cultural tradition of women narrating stories
with a visual aid

A Sculpted Sunrise

I sculpted a sunrise
on the shallows of
my body
it kissed my
breasts
trickled down
absences
lingering as rivulets
inside fractured furrows
of my veins

My galaxy awakened
from
an eclipsed ache, meteor
in rapid descent, tumbling
calcite as it paused
in presence
at vertebral edges
listening to echoes
of its own astral beginnings
a pulsing paraselene

I heard untangling
of my constellations
blazing
shards of names
inside my mouth
my tongue unfurling
languages unknown
I reached for your
impertinence, unstrung kites
falling into my apparitions

I leaned inside
you
and cinched
a fisherman's knot
of all my sputtering
aphrodite's
our tears in percussion
now quietened

quietened in waiting
to sculpt sunrise again
unfiltered

Children in Cages
after Martín Espada's Floaters

What else would you expect
of children in cages, playing
with balls and dolls, camps
turned into witness stands
they encourage the singing
of simple songs, gathering
their notes in soccer balls
and inside limbs of broken
dolls, they break back into
cages.
What else should we expect
of children in cages, waiting
too long.
simmering broth on her stove
she awaits, as shadows lengthen.
there is nothing to be done
a caged bird does not sing.

Transformation

crumbling anger
I see an icicle
melting

a caterpillar
dissolves itself
breaking free

water graves
grief washes ashore
in cockle shells

unclasped sky
a sidewalk sparkles
with snow

mountain peaks
just one breast remains
after surgery

a shimmering fish
learning the art
of letting go

Possibility

I let them be, scars as reminders
of your futility, how you often hurl
things at the sharp angles of my lissome body
and sometimes, the things you throw catch at edges
like bullets dodge themselves into dark vessels causing
them to bleed into breathless screams

I let them be, counting down
sustaining in bodies
barely alive.

you have continued to play
a game of severed sunsets
unperturbed
perhaps the stars will align
and change direction of a
sputtering earth.

I believe
hope will soon unfurl
in gentle petals, from
all who have departed
lost to isolated endings
hope will arrive, sporadic
in quietude if we let it. In.

origami

cradle songs
on the drive home…
my empty womb

my mother's
knitted sweaters
I unravel knots

tears
water raining into
an empty cup

drifting snowflakes
I restore the fragile lace
of my wedding veil

Code switching

Always exiting, appearances
Beyond
Coping
Drowning decomposed
Everyday engravings
Forced
Grieving
Howling herds
In symbolic
Juxtaposed
Kitchen smells
Last thoughts, land
Marriage vows
Nowhere, names
Opaque
Purged, of prayers, and playlists
Questions too
Reimagined
Sidewalks searched
Treasure hunts, tolerance
Undecided, documented, un
Velvet sounds
Wanderers, war zones
X name unknown when found
Your words
Zipped body bags

Woman by the Door

I sit by the door today
talk to myself

my voice quivers
as it reaches into the valley
where I had hidden you

I savor your ache, nuzzle you
swallow the leftover skies, of
canyons that were a fortress

I remember, in search for you
you smell of unfinished bread
pudding, the one mama made

       each morning, of caramelized
sugar
and
toasted
bread

I open the door and the silt
of the outside, storms inside
the tablecloth now drenched

A penance breaks dam, unease
arriving in tears, of all the years
you waited by windows, your

arms barricading them from
the storm that brewed inside
I descend into the wet walls
of your waiting cries, like an
explosion fluttering on sticky
butterfly wings.

metamorphosis, even a caterpillar
practices formlessness, then arrives
chitinous as a monarch. blanketed.

Curdled milk

he and I never succeed
in our attempt to mobilize
a conversation —
        about your death
all the light between our walls
fails to muscle through the
dark disconnectedness of our
cauterized veins, it flickers
like curdled milk simmering
on a stove, the conversation
lingers incoherently, neither
here nor there, delusional it
leaves a sour taste at the tip
of our tongues, our silence
settles to the bottom of the
pan, a weary landscape holds
all unfinished chunks, burnt
scraping the bowl for curds
and whey, a few lacerated
memories quiver in my hands
phantoms straining themselves
through the fine muslin of our
efforts, releasing palatable
emblems of memories that
consolidate into blocks of
neatly pressed paneer—

> a fresh memory of you becoming man, a wiry beard sprouting
> in a hurry, on days soft like cotton cand, others a wasteland
> another of you untangling your ever tangled laces, murmuring
> to yourself that favorite song, the words crackling like youth
> full of both song and dance, and then the repeat picture of
> you drowning in a biscuit cake, cheeks plastered, crumbs
> scraped off the plate, so much eaten and much distributed
> as if glucose biscuits, butter and cream had been whisked
> into beams of heaven itself, so blissful it always tasted, so
> blissful you always looked digging into it slice after slice.

when chopped it
mobilizes an aseptic conversation
that crumbles into a heated wok
cumin seeds splutter peacefully
he and I talk about your
death
here —
the boisterous storm
settles into a pale dawn.

Murmurs

astral lights
souls bide time
in fireflies

autumn night
beneath a quilt of leaves
the shadows shift

crescendo
cicadas mourn
in chorus

sleepless
an unlocked box
of needlework

a solitary moon
your presence
holds all seasons

yet another night
the hollowed cries
of a hemorrhage

Emptied Trees

That audacity
of scrawny legged birds
disappearing
as they slumber
in emptied trees
all wintered branches
parentless, swaying towards
the hierarchy of open ended
skies, its bluish grey
a moaning, nimble
mirror to the tumulus
below, a solitary birch
disrobing itself onto
rows of epitaphs
I turn away my stare
to listen to the *wit wit*
of a perched swallow.
It coaxes me to stay
inside the nectar of
her chorus, surrendering
I close my eyes holding
a half horizon inside.
A tree whistles an incantation.

Finding prayer

I try and find you in the words I say
those sent into the brass of the night
I lean into grief, edge of a mother's sob
where parts of prayers wait to be found

I heed the solace, that sits on treetops
even on nights that spirits laugh aloud
I become restless, like the river bend
stuttering quietly into broken rivulets

I wish to be the gilded revelry on wings
as sparrows gather their humble worms
I wonder about golden dandelions with
fingertips tenderly weeping in the wind

I listen to contradictory voices, focussing
on melancholy of 17th year cicada nymphs
I intend to beckon my body as it steps
into the trap door of luscious language

Stirrings

thanksgiving prayer
with grandparents-
flickering screen

festive season
I will miss you
every year

"grandpa calling"
my heart stops
beating

quiet afternoon
the empty swing
sways

dinner routine
keeping the tradition
of conversations

lingering aromas
grandmother's face
reflects in mine

newfound hobbies
sharing childhood stories
again, and again

still apart
I draw your ache
in my rainbows

buds unfurling
I wish some hope
would spill open

last light
a familiar horizon
fading away

disrobing
my own shadow
floating leaves

Cemetery paths

If a cemetery sang, even powdered snow would melt in remorse
If the dead talk, they would sing at sundown in many languages
If the pungent earth inside graves danced, stubbed grass will sway
If funeral ceremonies truly held ceremony, lies would live inside coffins
If letters on all tombstones were poems, then birds might perch longer
If the magnolia canopies stayed white, hope could bleach into bones
If a no moon night was less monosyllabic, I would sleep under the sky

Somewhere your grave will stay cradled in tears
Somewhere grief will enter cemeteries, bringing
a fistful of presence to leave behind on the paths
Somewhere a sparrow holds a spirit on her wings

Gratitude. | Shukr.

for the desire and practice

for body and being

for learning and teaching moments

for community of cheer leaders and conscience keepers – helping me get better and staying centered

for all who have read, chosen to publish and share these poems, thank you

for all who have not yet read but will read and offer their feedback and engagement

for all my early readers, you know who you are – I see your kindness

for Keki Sir – I am humbled beyond measure

for Kai Coggin – I am fortunate to have a place in your constellation

for Mumma, Papa – you bring poise to my being

for Sahir, Mansi, Sanah – you give me reason

for Manpreet – constantly constant

for everyone who knows of the lived experiences in these poems and can find resonance

for my gracious editor, Lynne Schmidt

for my committed publisher, Apprentice House Press and their capable, considerate team

for Dapindra – for seeing me even on the darkest days

for the steadfast attributes of sehaj, sehat and sabar

Acknowledgements

1. I Stopped counting – Poets Reading the News | November, 2019

2. My nana's video cassette library (*Now Nanapapa*) – Dream Noir | February, 2020

3. Half-finished poems (*Now Green Tea is only a Placebo*)– Inverse Journal | February, 2020

4. Country – Samyukta Poetry | August, 2020

5. Embroidered Tundra (*Now How a Woman delivers Hope*) – Madras Courier | October, 2020

6. Becoming Planets – Opiate Magazine | October, 2020

7. Normal – Rattle | November, 2020

8. Happiness Poems for the refrigerator – Alipore Post | November, 2020

9. Portrait of a Mother in America - Rising Phoenix Review | December, 2020

10. Ordinary Love – The Muse | December, 2020

11. Woman by the door – Silent World in her Vase | December, 2020

12. Hourglass – Silent World in her Vase | December, 2020

13. Questions (Now *Dendrochronology*) – Silent World in her Vase | December, 2020

14. Curdled milk – Narrow Road Journal | April, 2020, Yearbook of Indian Poets | 2021

15. All in a day – in 2020 – Ethel Zine | November, 2021

16. Cope – The Opiate Magazine | Volume 25, 2021

17. Your Lotus Gaze – Beltway Poetry Quarterly | 2021

18. A woman doing laundry – Takahe Magazine | 2021

19. Missing Questions – The Opiate Magazine | Volume 25

20. Turban/Pagri – Lucy Writer's Platform, 2020 and Yearbook of Indian poetry | 2021

21. A Sculpted sunrise – Shape of a Poem – An Anthology of Erotic poems | 2021

22. Confession – Upcoming in Bangalore Review | 2022

23. For the evil eye –North Dakota Review | Winter, 2021

24. Miracles – Rattle | November 2021

About the Author

When Kashiana is not writing, she lives to embody her TEDx talk theme of Work as Worship into her every day. She currently serves as poetry editor for *Poets Reading the News*.

Apprentice
House Press
Loyola University Maryland

Apprentice House is the country's only campus-based, student-staffed book publishing company. Directed by professors and industry professionals, it is a nonprofit activity of the Communication Department at Loyola University Maryland.

Using state-of-the-art technology and an experiential learning model of education, Apprentice House publishes books in untraditional ways. This dual responsibility as publishers and educators creates an unprecedented collaborative environment among faculty and students, while teaching tomorrow's editors, designers, and marketers.

Eclectic and provocative, Apprentice House titles intend to entertain as well as spark dialogue on a variety of topics. Financial contributions to sustain the press's work are welcomed. Contributions are tax deductible to the fullest extent allowed by the IRS.

To learn more about Apprentice House books or to obtain submission guidelines, please visit www.apprenticehouse.com.

Apprentice House
Communication Department
Loyola University Maryland
4501 N. Charles Street
Baltimore, MD 21210
410-617-5265
info@apprenticehouse.com
www.apprenticehouse.com

CPSIA information can be obtained
at www.ICGtesting.com
Printed in the USA
BVHW031550150222
629077BV00011B/661